THE MONTHLY RETAINER MODEL

THE MONTHLY RETAINER MODEL

IN FINANCIAL PLANNING

WHAT IT IS, WHY IT WORKS, & HOW TO IMPLEMENT IT IN YOUR FIRM

ALAN MOORE & MICHAEL KITCES

EDITED BY KALI HAWLK

Paperback ISBN: 978-0692769713

Cover and Book Design: Melody Christian, finickydesigns.com

CONTENTS

FOREWORD...1

ABOUT THE AUTHORS...5

CHAPTER 1: SETTING THE STAGE.............................7

CHAPTER 2: CHANGING YOUR BUSINESS MODEL TO SERVE GEN X AND GEN Y....................21

CHAPTER 3: HOW TO DESIGN YOUR OWN MONTHLY RETAINER MODEL FOR YOUR IDEAL CLIENTS...35

CHAPTER 4: IMPLEMENTING A MONTHLY RETAINER MODEL IN YOUR PRACTICE...................55

CHAPTER 5: DEALING WITH A MORE DIFFICULT SALE..67

CHAPTER 6: CASE STUDIES...............................77

CHAPTER 7: ADDITIONAL RESOURCES AND INFORMATION...99

FOREWORD

S top.

No really, stop.

Before you start reading this book, I need you to understand one very important thing deep down in your bones. I want you to feel it in your gut, because once you understand it, you'll change the world. Here it is: People need you!

You see, I've been conducting a little experiment where I ask people to describe for me how they feel about money in one word. The word that comes up over and over is anxiety. This has been true all over the United States, Canada, Europe, Australia, South Africa, and Asia. This same fear about money gets expressed to me in countless emails from readers of my New York Times column. People are worried. People are scared. In the U.S. alone, a recent Pew survey revealed that almost half of all Americans don't feel financially secure.[1] Among that group, over 83% worry about a lack of savings and almost 70% worry about not having enough money to retire. The numbers make it clear — people are scared. This has to change! People need *real* financial advice from *real* financial advisors now more than ever. But there's a problem.

People don't realize — or maybe they don't believe — that *real* financial advisors exist. All they know is what they hear on the financial pornography network, and the talking heads are marketing to a totally different group of people, and traditional financial industry has left this group behind.

And guess what? You are just the person to put an end to it because you belong to the Secret Society of Real Financial Advisors. You belong to this group because you've dedicated your professional life to serving people and helping them reach their goals. That said, your dedication comes with a catch.

You're so busy keeping your head down and doing the work that you don't exactly have a ton of time to figure out how to connect with the people who (desperately) need you. And remember, this group doesn't know you exist. They also tend to fall into an investing gap that the traditional financial industry keeps ignoring: people with only some money.

They want to save. They want to invest. But they don't hit the customary minimums, like $250,000, $500,000, or $1 million. So where do they go?

---

[1] http://www.pewtrusts.org/~/media/assets/2015/02/fsm-poll-results-issue-brief_artfinal_v3.pdf

Alan and Michael and the entire XY Planning Network believe they can and should come to you, and it starts with this book. This is your guide to working with people early on in their investing lives.

Alan and Michael also understand your desire to help people. It's why you chose this work, and they appreciate the need for a model that makes it possible for you to build a sustainable business in the process. Because, ultimately, the only way any of this changes is if you, my fellow members of the Secret Society, become less secret.

So as you dive into this book, I want you to keep that one thing in mind: People need you! They need you not only for your technical expertise, but also for your ability to stand between them and the stupid things we humans do when it comes to money.

Alan, Michael, and the XYPN team have given you the roadmap. Now, it's up to you to follow it.

Carl Richards

CERTIFIED FINANCIAL PLANNER™

Author of *The Behavior Gap* and *The One-Page Financial Plan*

Sketch Guy columnist for The New York Times and columnist for Morningstar Advisor

ABOUT THE AUTHORS

Alan Moore, MS, CFP® is the co-founder of the XY Planning Network and is the Champion of NextGen at Abacus Wealth Partners, a fee-only RIA and financial planning firm managing over $1.5 billion AUM.

He is passionate about helping financial planners start and grow their own fee-only firms to serve Gen X & Gen Y clients largely ignored by traditional firms. Alan has been recognized by Investment News as a top "40 Under 40" in financial planning, and by Wealth Management as one of a "The 10 to Watch in 2015. He frequently speaks on topics related to technology, marketing, and business coaching, and has been quoted in publications including The Wall Street Journal, Forbes and The New York Times.

 **Michael Kitces, MSFS, MTAX, CFP®, CLU, ChFC, RHU, REBC, CASL,** is a co-founder of the XY Planning Network, the practitioner editor of the Journal of Financial Planning, and the publisher of the e-newsletter The Kitces Report and the popular financial planning industry blog Nerd's Eye View.

Michael is an active writer and editor across the industry and has been featured in publications including Financial Planning, the Journal of Financial Planning, Journal of Retirement Planning, as well as The Wall Street Journal, BusinessWeek, CNBC PowerLunch, NBC Nightly News, and more.

Michael is one of the 2010 recipients of the Financial Planning Association's "Heart of Financial Planning" awards for his dedication to advancing the financial planning profession.

CHAPTER 1:
SETTING THE STAGE

It's time to address something all financial advisors know to be true, but most don't usually admit. The financial planning industry is slow to change and slow to adopt new practices, new technology, and new marketing techniques. It doesn't matter if you look at investment management, insurance sales, or true financial planning. In any view, it's easy to see that we're stuck in old ways of doing things simply because that's the way it's always been done. One only has to look to other industries to see just how far behind we are.

There are many reasons why we're stuck. We haven't needed to change, since our businesses are profitable. We haven't seen the technological innovations that many other industries have experienced, because advisors typically do not purchase new technology (which discourages technology innovation in our space). Neither businesses nor individuals invest much in technology designed for running financial planning practices.

Not to mention, ours is a highly regulated industry. That regulation and strict requirements to stick to existing standards tends to slow technology innovation. It certainly slows individual advisors and firm owners from taking risks by adopting that new technology — especially if there are any regulatory gray areas that the industry hasn't yet resolved.

Additionally, we have an aging generation of advisors. While this older group of advisors created what financial planning is today, they're still operating the same way they ran businesses and served clients a decade or so ago. And little wonder: technically, it's been working. These advisors and their firms have been making money, so why push change? Why push for progress when the same old thing seems to keep bringing money in the door?

But we're starting to see many things happening at once in the financial planning industry. The landscape is changing, whether individual advisors and their practices are okay with it or not. The profession as a whole is evolving from where the industry began.

You can divide the history of our profession into three stages. The first starts with financial advisors getting paid for selling products. This transitioned to financial advisors getting paid for managing portfolios. The third stage is the one we're in the midst of now, in which advisors are paid for financial planning itself.

THE CHANGING LANDSCAPE OF FINANCIAL PLANNING

Financial planning became popular because it was a more effective means to sell products. Financial advisors were stock brokers and insurance agents; financial planning was an opportunity to better understand someone's needs so that you could sell them a product or service to match their needs.

This first stage of the industry worked for many years until technology scaled the cost to trade stocks and bonds. This dropped transaction costs (and potential stockbroker commissions) by almost 90% in 20 years from the mid 1970s to mid 1990s. Advisors were forced to move up the value chain.

The second stage of the industry began here, and we saw the rise of the assets under management model. Advisors became asset gatherers who realized that, while financial planning is also good for selling products, it's also great for selling, building, and deepening relationships with the clients whose money they manage on an ongoing basis.

The AUM model wasn't the real start of getting paid for financial planning, but it did deliver financial planning in a manner that wasn't necessarily sales- and product-centric. The assets under management fee structure shifted the focus from products and sales, to asset management and relationships.

Today, we're witnessing another evolution in our industry. Financial planning is provided as a service for the sake of financial planning — not as an add-on or a "free" bonus for investment management clients. If you're still trying to only sell products in an increasingly advice-centric world, it's incredibly difficult to show your value as an advisor because any consumer who just wants the products can go online and buy them directly.

And consumers are beginning to understand the difference between advice and sales. Whether caused by debates of the fiduciary rule in the Department of Labor that sparked a media frenzy, or simply because a Google search makes any and all information exponentially more accessible, consumers are beginning to recognize that there is a difference.

Nobody likes a salesperson and nobody wants to be sold. And so salespeople are increasingly finding it difficult to compete.

But in this changing landscape, it's not enough to move away from being a salesperson and start being a true advisor. As more and more advisors become advice centric, the new challenge is to differentiate yourself from everyone else who is part of the movement to get paid for financial planning as a service onto itself. This drives what we like to call the "crisis of differentiation," which we'll talk more about in Chapters 3 and 5.

THE INDUSTRY'S CLIENTS ARE CHANGING, TOO

As the financial planning industry has changed, so too have the clients of industry professionals. Advisors today largely serve Baby Boomers, and people with assets who are approaching retirement or transitioning into a traditional retirement. The dominant fee structure has been AUM, which requires a client to actually have assets for the advisor to manage. This lends itself to older clients that actually have money saved. But the advisor who wants to be successful tomorrow needs to understand a new client who looks very different than the Boomers.

There are two primary distinctions most advisors see in the next generations of financial planning clients. (By next generation, we're referring to Gen X and Gen Y, traditionally defined as people born between 1965 and 1979 and 1980 and 1990, respectively.) The most basic difference is that these generations are at a different life stage. They're not at the stage of retirement. They're in their 20s at their youngest and 50s at the oldest. Retirement is pretty far out in their minds because it's *literally* pretty far out on the timelines of their lives. The day they'll stop working may be 20 or 30 or even 40 years into the future.

But this just isn't relevant for the next generation of clients. It's just not where they are from a life stage perspective.

Nevermind the fact that members of Gen X and Gen Y have increasingly come into the workforce carrying more debt than previous generations. As of 2015, Americans hold $1.23 trillion dollars in student loan debt.[2] The only larger debt level is mortgages, which many Gen X & Gen Y clients are also taking on. They're also experiencing a completely different work dynamic once they get there. They experience more job changes and far fewer periods of long-term employment with one company. Gen X and Gen Y must take on more responsibility for saving on their own because the rise of defined contribution plans and the decline in defined pension plans.

The second primary distinction that begins to define the change in the next generation of clients is the fact that they have different expectations around what a financial advisor is going to do for them. They find different services more relevant and maintain a different understanding of what experience to expect from their advisor. With information easily available on the Internet, advisors are no longer the holders of all the insider knowledge. Most of the knowledge advisors possess can be found on Google, with a good enough search and a dedicated enough searcher. Of course, much like WebMD didn't replace the doctor, Google won't replace the advisor. But it *is* forcing a change in the relationship advisors have with their clients, which we see being even more prevalent among younger clients and their advisors.

When financial planning began as a profession, advisors were product salespeople. We were insurance agents or stock brokers. And we did some financial planning

---

[2] https://www.nerdwallet.com/blog/credit-card-data/average-credit-card-debt-household/

because it was a good way to demonstrate the need for the products that we had to sell, but sales remained our focus.

Young people today increasingly are looking to financial advisors. They take the title literally and actually expect advice. They're looking for help planning their financial lives. Products are something that they can buy online themselves, but advice is something Gen X and Gen Y clients seek out from a human being they can have a conversation with; a website can give us information, but it can't tell us how to apply it to our lives.

But the *way* next generation clients expects to receive that advice is different, too. That's particularly true for for Gen Y, also known as Millennials, and considered digital natives. Gen Y grew up in a world of digital technology that supported their communication interactions. As a result, the whole idea of meeting face-to-face to look over paper reports is either an alien concept or something that's considered completely unnecessary and a waste of time. They prefer to consume content in a digital, virtual environment if a digital, virtual environment is faster and more convenient.

Next-generation clients are often savvier in general because of their comfort level with technology and their native knowledge on how to find the information they want. We're starting to see clients come to us who know how advisors charge and how much money financial planners make. They know the difference between commission and fee-only. They're more educated and can ask more probing questions about fiduciary standards and whether or not you'll work for them under that standard. Of course, not all clients are this well educated. But the information is out there and available, and distinctions in the industry are no longer reserved as insider information as they once might have been.

Gen X and Gen Y clients are also looking for a specific kind of advisor. They know they're looking for financial planning and comprehensive financial advice, not just insurance sales. Younger clients are looking for advisors who speak their language and understand their life stage. They want specialists to serve their specific interests, needs, and goals.

Let's consider the craft beer industry as an analogy to better understand these ideas.

Consider how big, corporate players used to dominate. There was no room on the shelves for small-time operations between products from Budweiser, Coors, and Miller. But in recent years, there's been a huge demand — especially among Gen X and Gen Y demographics — for what's known as craft beer. Younger generations tend to prefer locally made, locally sourced, specialty beers, and shun products from bigger, national companies that are generic, plain, and mass produced. Today's consumers want unique and different offerings from the beer industry, and they're interested in very specific kinds of tastes and flavors.

This move away from big, broad, and general products with a corporate feel and toward smaller, niched-down, and personal is happening in financial planning as well. It's driven by the desires of the same consumer segment who want to feel like the companies they work with and give their money to actually care about their experiences and needs. They don't want faceless corporations or to feel distant from their service providers.

Consider, from a sales perspective, what happens if we create a specialty beer (or a specialty service) that has a really unique profile that only appeals to a really small subset of people — but the people that it *does* appeal to are raving fans because it's perfect for them. This is what's possible right now. You can develop a niche and reach a specific group of people that don't need to be sold on your offering, because they're naturally attracted to it and they know it's what they want.

Today's financial planning clients want specialists who service people in a very specific situation. They want the expert in their unique needs. Previous generations didn't hire advisors this way. They would hire the advisor that lived closest to them, that handled their parents' finances, or worked at the local bank. We never really had specialists in financial planning, but it's becoming necessary because today's clients are different.

Going forward through the rest of this book for the sake of use as you read, we'll lump Gen X and Gen Y together and call them the "next generation." It's worth noting, however, that Gen X and Gen Y are extremely different generations. (It's also simply not fair to act as if all members of a generation are the same.)

WHY BOTHER WITH GEN X AND GEN Y, ANYWAY?

You get it: next-generation clients are different. But why bother with servicing their needs, if those needs are so incompatible with the way the industry currently is?

There are many reasons for financial advisors to focus on Gen X and Gen Y clients. Some of it is simply a long term strategy play. Gen X and Gen Y clients who don't necessarily have significant income and wealth now *will* accumulate wealth over time. If you want to really connect with next-generation clients, or you want to build a pipeline of future affluent clients, that means creating an efficient, profitable way to serve less affluent clients now and grow with them.

This is notable because the reality is almost all of the established advisory firms around today didn't launch by getting wealthy clients from the start. They launched by getting less wealthy clients — often *younger* clients. And the advisors that started today's flagship firms were younger when they started, too, and worked with their peers. They turned their friends and peers with $50,000 accounts into millionaire clients by growing with them over time.

Working with Gen X and Gen Y clients is simply a long-term strategy for growing, developing, and sustaining a successful business. More and more parts of the industry are recognizing this fact. We believe this is why we're currently seeing large asset managers, custodians, and broker-dealers encouraging advisors toward Gen X and Gen Y clients. There's acknowledgement from those firms that, if they want to be around and relevant for 20 to 30 years, they need their advisors to be building connections to next generation clients now.

But beyond being a strategy for long-term growth and success, serving younger clients provides you with a huge opportunity for growth right now. Financial planning for next-generation clients is such an untapped marketplace! Because Gen X and Gen Y clients have the income but not the wealth or assets to buy a lot of traditional financial planning products, and they certainly don't have the wealth to meet the traditional AUM model, they're an underserved segment in the industry.

Profitably serving Gen X and Gen Y does require a different business model than what we've traditionally used. Selling products doesn't work. Neither does AUM, because younger individuals don't have assets under management yet. This becomes a question of "how do you actually build a viable, sustainable, profitable fee-for-service model to serve younger clients that sees them as profitable today and not just in the distant future?"

The answer? Implementing the monthly retainer model, or said another way, doing financial planning for a monthly subscription fee. Next generation clients can afford the fee because they have the income (even if they don't have the assets), so they're capable and willing to pay for advice. The monthly retainer model is a viable, long-term solution that provides recurring revenue to allow advisors to create a profitable business today *and* into the future.

In a world where so few advisors are serving Gen X and Gen Y clients, and virtually none of them with this new business model, the monthly retainer model provides a huge opportunity. Everyone else is trying to retrofit Gen X and Gen Y into existing models. They're saying, "hey, I'll manage your assets but I'll do it at a discount since you don't have much to manage."

We call this playing the client lottery. Firms work with 20 younger clients with little in assets with the hope that one or two of them have rich parents that die and leave them money, making their lottery play profitable.

And these clients see right through this strategy. They want comprehensive financial planning. They don't want you to give them some trimmed down version of financial planning, or "financial planning lite." They don't want you to push products.

It's a wide open arena – or a "blue ocean" market – because no one else is serving this space. This is completely unlike competing for Baby Boomer clients. As a market, this demographic is a messy "red ocean." In that market, you compete with almost every other financial advisor who goes after the same type of client.

The Blue Ocean Strategy is a business book that breaks markets into two groups: red oceans and blue oceans. Red oceans are identified by fierce competition, in which there are many market players and services are essentially commoditized. Red oceans are notable because over time, fighting over the same select marketplace forces sellers to compete on price — and that's a market no business wants to be in. The name "red ocean" comes from the metaphor that there are many sharks in the water, tearing at each other for the same buyers. Blue oceans, on the other hand, are untapped markets. There are few market players and limited competition. Service providers get to create a service model that caters to the clients they want to serve without being forced to commoditize their service and compete solely on price. All business owners want to be in the blue ocean.

Serving Gen X and Gen Y instead of older generation clients is the perfect example of a blue ocean market in financial planning.

If you're ready to explore the monthly retainer model to serve next-generation individuals, this is your opportunity to acquire young clients who you can grow with for the long run as they eventually accumulate wealth and assets. It's also your opportunity to serve them profitably *today*.

Our goal for this book is equip you with the tools to go out and design a service model to work with younger clients. But a word of caution. This isn't some minor tweak to your firm. This isn't, "let's just make a couple of changes here and there" and suddenly Gen X and Gen

Y clients will show up at your doorstep. Serving the next generation of client will require a wholesale change in your business model. Nothing in your current process will go untouched. If you're not committed to creating a business model that works for these clients, you won't survive the changes that are necessary.

All that being said, it's important to keep in mind that there is *no* reason to work with Gen X and Gen Y clients if you don't want to. You don't *have* to in order to find success as a financial advisor. There are opportunities here, both for the short- and long-term, but you need a passion for working with younger clients and helping them with situations that they are dealing with, that their parents or grandparents are not dealing with, if you want to have success.

Younger clients are dealing with issues like student loans, cash flow, debt management, buying houses, having babies, getting married, getting divorced, starting businesses – all things that Baby Boomer and retired clients generally don't deal with (and certainly not all at once). Don't work with next generation clients just because you think they're going to inherit money. Work with them because you believe that they need your help and you're the best advisor to help them.

CHAPTER 2:
CHANGING YOUR BUSINESS MODEL TO SERVE GEN X AND GEN Y

C reating a service model to serve Gen X and Gen Y clients requires rethinking and completely restructuring the way your firm generates revenue. Instead of looking at existing business structures and trying to make it fit for the next generation, go back and ask this question: "If we were building this from the ground up, how would we design a fee structure to work with Gen X and Gen Y clients?"

Assets under management (AUM) is simply not an option if you want to serve this demographic profitably. We can do the math to see that, ultimately, you can't generate revenue on an AUM basis if you're working with clients that don't have assets. Most next-generation clients don't have assets — and if they do, those assets are usually tied up in 401(k)s or equity in their homes.

Even if someone in their 20s, 30s, or 40s has a net worth that makes them look like a viable client, they may not have enough liquid assets in an investable account for you as the advisor to manage and deduct 1% of fees to run a profitable business.

And you *should* get paid to serve these clients. No one is asking advisors to work pro-bono. We don't run charities. It's not sustainable to try and build a business around serving "poor" clients today in the hopes they'll be "rich" someday in the future.

It is perfectly fine to charge for the services that you're rendering and get paid to do that work. But that means you must find a model that balances both sides of the equation: you can serve Gen X and Gen Y in a way that is affordable to them, *and* in a way that's profitable for you.

THE NEW BUSINESS MODEL THAT WORKS FOR NEXT GENERATION CLIENTS

Charging assets under management worked for clients with assets to manage. It made sense and worked well for all parties. But this model fails with next generation clients who have the income to pay for advice, but not the assets on which the advisor can charge a commission on.

When advisors say, "I can't work with younger clients because they don't have any assets to manage and therefore they aren't profitable to my firm," what they're actually expressing is that the existing service model and fee structure designed for different types of clients with assets does not work for clients without assets. And we agree! We can all do the math to understand that as a business owner, you can't profitably run your firm by serving clients that have an average of $50,000 in an IRA when you charge 1% AUM.

But this isn't a client problem. It's a business model problem. If we could be free from the expectations and the history — and the "way things have always been done" mindset — we could then openly ask questions like:

How can we build a fee structure to serve younger clients?

How does that fee structure function so clients can afford the services and advisors can make a profit?

We asked these questions and landed on the monthly retainer model as the answer. No, this isn't the way it's always been done. No, business has not normally been done this way. But the monthly retainer model works both for next generation clients and for the advisors who want to serve them while still running a business that can generate revenue.

It's important to understand that we did not set out to cut fees for young clients. It's not about making financial planning cheaper (and AUM is not "too expensive" for clients). We do believe that you cannot run a profitable business that serves Gen X and Gen Y clients and charge assets under management for those clients. They may not have those assets, but they do have the income to pay you monthly. So let's set up that fee structure and teach others how to, as well.

THE ADVANTAGES OF THE MONTHLY RETAINER MODEL

One of the biggest advantages of the monthly retainer model is that it enables financial advisors to work with clients much earlier in their life, and to therefore engage with clients for a longer period of time. Instead of limiting your client pool to the traditional market of people in their 50s, 60s, 70s, and older who already built wealth and provide assets to manage, using a retainer model allows you to profitably plan for people in their 20s, 30s, and 40s. And there are a wealth of planning opportunities for people in this age range. Life in these decades can be extremely dynamic with many changes — most of which are tied to financial decisions for which these clients need advice.

The monthly retainer model makes financial planning more accessible to more people. That provides opportunities both for them and, of course, for you as a business owner serving clients.

There are a variety of other advantages, too. Consider the following:

CREATE TRANSPARENT PRICING

This is something some advisors might say they *don't* want to do, but ultimately the marketplace is moving toward a fiduciary standard and more transparency on pricing and fees. There's more and more openly available information online that shows consumers exactly how much they are paying for financial planning. Consumers then get to evaluate if it makes sense for them to continue to pay for the service.

This is obviously great for the consumer, but can present a challenge for some advisors. Transparent pricing requires you to understand, believe, and communicate the value of your services. The monthly fee will be less than the value you likely provide when you consider what you're doing for your clients. You could improve cash flow to save money, change insurance policies to more appropriate products, or invest wisely to grow wealth for the people you work with. But you need to clearly and adequately explain your value to prospects and clients.

(In Chapter 5, we'll explain a few tips and strategies for dealing with a more difficult "sale" and communicating your value.)

CREATE DISTINCTION BETWEEN SERVICES

Historically, financial advisors have charged a percentage of investments as an AUM fee — and we have thrown in financial planning for free. This created a problem: it was hard for financial advisors to really dedicate focus and resources to financial planning when they were charging the same fee regardless of whether they really did any financial planning or not.

But when an advisor's core business model is to get paid for financial planning, the advisor has a real incentive to focus on making it as valuable and well-executed as possible. It's the essence of the business!

Charging a monthly fee and tacking on investment management as a separate AUM charge allows you to clearly distinguish what you offer. You create two separate fees for two separate services. And to an earlier point, this also allows you to provide investment management without asset minimums, since it allows you to be profitable on the financial planning side (assuming that you've designed your fee structure in a way that makes you profitable).

CREATE THE BOND IN YOUR FIRM'S FEE INCOME PORTFOLIO

We can all remember back in 2008 and 2009 when AUM-only firms lost 15% to 30% of their revenue within a few quarters. That was devastating from a business perspective. Even companies running a healthy 20% or 25% margin were stung by the volatility and extreme downturn in the market. Advisors needed to manage businesses with profits that were dropping and simultaneously deal with panicked clients. The market crash hurt everyone, but AUM-only firms dealt with a particularly messy situation.

An AUM-only business model bases the revenue of a financial planning firm on something advisors cannot control: the markets. Even if you believe that you can generate some alpha in the marketplace, you can't control your profits when the market drops 40%. Even when the revenue eventually comes back when markets even out, it creates tough sledding for AUM-only firms in the interim.

Flat monthly fees, on the other hand, are flat no matter what. The monthly retainer model is not dependent on the market. It's a predictable, recurring revenue source into your firm. So consider the monthly retainer model like the "bond" in your income portfolio, and think about the AUM side of the house as the "stock" that's a little more volatile. Revenues tied to AUM will go up — and they will go down. Flat monthly fees generated by your monthly retainer model will stay flat.

THE DISADVANTAGES TO THE MONTHLY RETAINER MODEL

There are plenty of benefits and advantages to implementing a monthly retainer model in your practice. But there are downsides, too, and it's important to understand the disadvantages before implementing this model into your financial planning firm. If you're aware of the challenges, you can be better equipped to handle them when adding a monthly retainer to your business model.

Payment Processing

While it sounds easy to bill clients on a monthly basis, actually receiving payment for your monthly fee is challenging. Broker dealers have made it difficult to charge for activities they can't oversee. They're hesitant to allow the processing of payments on a monthly basis. (Broker dealers may also be hesitant to allow financial planning done monthly in general, because they must monitor that their advisors are actually providing service and value that justifies the monthly fee.)

Credit card companies and banks can also be hesitant to work with financial advisors. Paypal and Intuit Quickbooks, along with other processors, have all expressly stated that they do not want to work with financial advisors and exclude many financial services from their terms of acceptable use[3]. And if you're working with a broker dealer, most of them do not have a way for you to charge a monthly fee. There are certainly hurdles to overcome, but you *can* get paid on a monthly basis.

To get around this problem, some advisors will have their clients set up automatic bill pay from their bank to mail the

---

[3] http://quickbooks.intuit.com/legal/payments/acceptable-use

advisor a check on a monthly basis. While this is workable, it can create a headache because the advisor must cash all the checks and chase down clients. Other, more efficient ways include using systems like FreshBooks paired with Authorize.net, but there are concerns that have yet to be answered around PCI compliance, ability to make changes to clients recurring bill payments without their express permission, and more.

State regulators have also started asking more questions regarding the feature sets of payment processors to ensure advisors are following not only the letter of the law when it comes to potentially triggering custody, but also the spirit of the law in that clients have enough access to information and flexibility with features to ensure they are not taken advantage of.

AdvicePay, a payment processing company created specifically to help financial advisors running the monthly retainer model, offers a solution that is easy to use *and* compliant. Read more about AdvicePay in the next section of this chapter.

Too Much Transparency?

While we *are* huge fans of pricing transparency, it *does* put the money that we are charging clients in the client's' face. They are paying a fee every single month for financial planning. Every single month, they get to ask the question, "am I getting value from my financial advisor?" (Again, we talk more about different ways to show value on an on-going monthly basis in later chapters.)

Raising Fees Over Time

When you set a monthly fee, you also set an expectation for clients who accept the cost. Flat fees are wonderful at times, especially in down markets. But those same fees present a challenge in up markets. The costs to run a firm inflate over time, while fees are "sticky" in the clients' mind and hard to raise. If advisors fail to plan for this challenge and find ways to increase fees over time (that work for their clients), it can create margin pressure in the long run. You must have an up-front strategy for a problem that will quietly grow over time if not addressed.

A NEW SOLUTION FOR COMPLIANT PAYMENT PROCESSING: ADVICEPAY

AdvicePay is the first ever payment processor built specifically for the needs of financial advisors. Our industry falls under an immense amount of regulation on how we process money from clients. When we first launched the XY Planning Network, we worked with payment processors to develop a custom feature set specifically for financial advisors. But most of those efforts fizzled out; there was a lack of interest in developing industry specific features. To finally provide a way for advisors to easily handle monthly billing, we built a custom payment processor specifically for financial advisors. We developed and launched AdvicePay to handle the needs of advisors charging on a monthly basis, keep RIAs compliant, and provide an easy-to-use payment process for both advisors and clients.

One of the main features of the service is that it avoids triggering custody of client funds. Some regulators deem having a voided check or credit card numbers enough to trigger custody — meaning they ruled that with those items, advisors have enough access to client funds to steal from their client.[4]

Maintaining custody comes with many burdens for an RIA. For example, if an advisor is deemed to have custody, they must adhere to a requirement for an annual "surprise" audit by an independent public accountant (at the advisor's expense) to verify client assets, which costs a minimum of $10,000. Other payment processors have raised the concerns of regulators around issues of what counts as advisors having custody.

AdvicePay was built to *not* trigger custody, or even to have the option or feature set that might allow you as the advisor to trigger custody. It was also created to provide advisors with the ability to do recurring billing and one-time billing, using either credit cards or ACH.

Here's a set of questions one particular state regulator wanted addressed around payment processing services for advisors:

- Who initially sets the amount of money to be withdrawn, and the frequency? Client or advisor?

---

[4] https://www.kitces.com/blog/having-client-passwords-and-other-ways-an-ria-may-fail-to-avoid-the-sec-custody-rule/

- Does client have ability to change and/or cancel the amounts and frequency of payments independent of advisor knowledge?

- For the sake of transparency, does the client have 24/7 access and ability to view transactions, statements, and so on? Do they have a portal they can access at any time?

- Does the client pay any fees to the payment processor to use the service?

AdvicePay was designed with the questions in mind. Here are the answers:

- The advisor sets up the payment information, but it is approved by the client.

- The client can change and/or cancel the amounts and frequency of payments independent of advisor knowledge. The client can log in to delete their recurring billing, change payment account, and more — without contacting the advisor.

- The client has access to their account and settings at all times.

- The client does not pay any fee to AdvicePay to use the service.

How AdvicePay Works

AdvicePay is an ideal solution for you if you're looking to charge clients using credit cards or ACH on a one-time or recurring basis — which is the preferred payment method of anyone running a monthly retainer model in their financial planning firm.

Here's a quick walkthrough example of how AdvicePay works once you sign up:

- Log into the portal and see your account at any time.

- Set up a new client using their name and e-mail.

- Choose one of the following options: send a one-time invoice; set up a new recurring plan for the client; assign client to an existing subscription plan

- The client then receives an e-mail that asks them to create a username and password on the AdvicePay platform and set up their banking information. The client will then approve the one-time payment or subscription billing.

In AdvicePay, clients always maintain the ability to cancel their subscription, see all previous invoices, see any upcoming payments, and store their payment info to easily pay one-time invoices as needed. And advisors can always access a dashboard to see all clients in one place, view and manage a list of all errors (such as failed payments, late invoices, and so on), and review a list of all actions a client has taken in the system. All actions are tracked and downloadable for regulates and/or CCO review.

Why AdvicePay for Advisors Using the Monthly Retainer Model?

In the current landscape, payment processor choices for financial advisors running a monthly retainer model are very limited. Systems like Quickbooks Intuit Merchant Accounts specifically forbid all financial services from using their service (including the XY Planning Network itself — which isn't even a financial services firm, but works with folks in financial services). Any advisor using it can be removed without notice, which would be a logistical nightmare.

Other systems like PaySimple provide too much flexibility for regulators to agree that the service is completely compliant. The issue is with features like the ability to change a client's monthly billing amount without their approval. Regulators are starting to look more closely at features like this, and are classifying them as situations in which the advisor has custody.

Because AdvicePay does not give advisors custody of funds, provides transparency for both advisors and clients, and allows clients to change information and cancel payments at any time without needing to go through their advisor, it's an ideal service if you're looking to get paid for financial planning services on a monthly subscription basis.

CHAPTER 3: HOW TO DESIGN YOUR OWN MONTHLY RETAINER MODEL FOR YOUR IDEAL CLIENTS

You're convinced: you want to implement a monthly retainer model in your financial planning practice. But where do you start? Designing and implementing this fee structure into a firm that provides comprehensive financial planning isn't as easy as choosing an AUM-only model for a firm focusing on investment management first (with financial planning advice as a tacked-on freebie).

A financial planning firm offering comprehensive planning services must clearly define what those services are. From there, you can develop a monthly subscription fee for clients to pay that is in line with the value of the services you offer. Here's how to think through this and design your own retainer model that allows clients to gain access to that comprehensive planning you provide.

First, you need to understand who you want to reach, who you want to work with, and what you'll offer that particular group of people. At XY Planning Network, we usually talk about "serving Gen X and Gen Y clients." But even within that category, that's an incredibly wide range of diverse people.

The needs of someone in their 40s with two children and a mortgage who is focused on climbing up the corporate ladder will be different than a single person in their 20s who just got their first real job and carries thousands of dollars in student loan debt. And the needs of both those people will be radically different than those of someone in their 30s going through a job change while preparing to get married or start a family.

People will have different needs based on age, but also on life stage, location, profession, employment status, income level, net worth, and so on. This means there are a million different options for the segment of the market you can serve. And who you want to work with is a critical starting point because it dictates what you ultimately do for your clients.

FIND YOUR CLIENT NICHE

If you decide that your goal is to specialize in young lawyers who are on a track to partnerships at their firms, you may want to become the country's leading expert in how attorneys negotiate partnership deals in their businesses. Or let's say you decide you want to serve folks who are employees and getting a salary plus employee benefits. You can specialize in knowing how to help you clients with employee benefits and 401(k) elections. You can even specialize in these services specifically for employees of one particular corporation.

This way of thinking provides a completely different, niche-based solution that is relevant to those ideal clients, but not anyone else. If you don't know who you're serving, then you won't know what specialized solutions you can offer that allow you to stand out from the crowd. That will make it difficult to design a specific monthly retainer model (from a list of services to exact fees for those services) for your firm *and* to sell your value to clients.

Understanding specific needs and goals of your clients will allow you to figure out what you'll offer to those people, and make it easy to create what we call a "client service calendar." You can fill this in with actual, specific, concrete services you'll provide for the clients throughout the year.

But before you get too carried away in dreaming up the specialized services you can provide and wow your specific segment of clients with, you need to ensure you're on the right page. And the easiest way to do this is to actually talk with people who fall into your desired niche. Starting a conversation opens a window onto what this group needs, wants, expects, and can afford. Getting to know the kind of people you want to serve in this way provides a wonderful opportunity to nail down exactly how you'll serve your niche.

CONDUCT COFFEE MEETINGS (AKA: MODERN MARKET RESEARCH)

Find about a dozen people in your target niche. Approach them and invite them to join you for an informal meeting. You might say something like, "I'm trying to craft a business that is relevant for people like you. I would love to take you out for coffee and get your advice on the issues or challenges there are in your world."

You want to have a conversation that gives you insight into the problems and pain points that your ideal client experiences — that you work to solve with your service offering.

At the meeting, you can ask questions like:

- "What type of financial struggles do you have?"

- "What sorts of services, if I'm trying to craft a business, are relevant for someone like you?"

- "What kind of solutions do I need to provide for you to feel like there's value in working together?"

- "What would you be *willing* to pay for a financial planner who specializes in your exact situation? What *can* you actually afford?"

Then, listen and take notes. The goal is not to sell them on anything or pitch them on anything at all! Your goal is to simply ask questions about their needs and challenges, and listen. See what they come back with and start to formulate what's relevant.

After talking with a dozen people, you'll almost certainly hear common challenges, themes, ideas, goals; common areas of financial life that are really relevant for your niche. The answers to your questions, and what's common across the people you interview, can become the nucleus of the service offering you deliver to your clients in your financial planning practice.

This gives you a starting point, but your work here isn't through. Before you conclude your first meeting, be sure to ask if it's okay to follow up in the future. You can say something like, "I'm going to interview several other people too, and I'd like to come back to you in a month or so to share what I've come up with. It would be great if you could tell me if it seems reasonable or not. Would it be okay to follow-up in the future for one more lunch meeting?"

Most people will agree. When you meet again, share what you came up with throughout your first round of interviews. Explain the themes you found and the price points you came up with. Ask if your services are relevant, and if the price for them is reasonable. Your interviewees will either confirm and say you're on the right track — or they'll point out what's irrelevant or missing.

> You may find a few of the people you met for coffee are going to say that the business you're trying to build would be perfect for themselves. In that moment, you have an opportunity to say "That's great! And I'd actually love to work with you sometime." You'll find that a few people say yes, and those will be your first clients.

WHAT SHOULD YOU CHARGE FOR YOUR SERVICES?

Once you've determined your niche and developed a service offering for your ideal clients, your next step to implement a monthly retainer in your practice is to nail down what you'll charge. That begins with understanding what people can realistically pay *and* what they will pay. Remember, your coffee meetings lay a solid groundwork here (so don't skip that important step of actually speaking to the kind of people you think you want to work with!).

What your ideal clients can pay is related not only to income and needs, but also to job and context. If you're going to work with younger teachers, they might be able to only afford $100 per month. If you're going to work with entre-preneurs in their 40s who already sold a successful company and are trying to figure out what to do with the rest of their lives, $500 per month could be completely reasonable.

Ultimately, something that creates high value justifies a higher price point. If the initial client services calendar you create demands a high monthly fee that your clients don't want to pay or simply can't pay, you may need to consider adjusting those services. Offer less or scale back in some way so that your services align with the fee you charge — and that fee makes sense for the specific group of people you want as clients.

Even if the service is otherwise valuable for the cost, the business won't work if your niche clientele just can't afford it.

THE THREE TYPES OF PRICING IN A MONTHLY RETAINER MODEL

In general, pricing in the monthly retainer model follows one of three structures: the monthly subscription fee, the upfront fee, and "add-on" fees.

The monthly subscription (or retainer, or service) fee is the flat fee clients will pay each month for ongoing services with you. This could be anywhere from $50 per month to $200 or more. Again, this fee depends on the service you offer and the client you serve.

Note that throughout this book, we do refer to this part of the fee as the "monthly retainer," but this is industry jargon. We highly recommend using the term "subscription fee" when speaking with clients.

The upfront fee is different from the monthly retainer. It is a one-time fee that you charge when you initially engage with a client.

You could call this an onboarding fee, project fee, or initial planning fee. Regardless of what you name it, this fee is important to consider for your business and acknowledge with clients if you implement it. The upfront fee recognizes the amount of upfront work that may be involved in the initial planning relationship.

And an upfront fee is a commitment device. This weeds out those who aren't truly serious about planning and would likely have hired you, but then dropped off quickly. When someone has to pay a significant sum of money up front but isn't dedicated, they'll balk and will self-select out of your sales pipeline. This saves you time, energy, and work on a client who would have been a poor fit for your practice. Anyone willing to pay an upfront planning fee is much more likely to follow through and be committed to the process.

The third fee you may want to include in your service model is the add-on fees. These are additional services provided at an hourly rate or for a flat project fee.

You can offer to work for $X per hour on issues for clients who don't need comprehensive planning and only need your advice on a specific element of their finances. This allows you to say, "if we have additional work that goes above a certain threshold or limit that's outside the scope of my normal agreement, I can still help." You can provide the service but protect the value of your ongoing monthly fee.

Or you can develop that flat fee package or project. You can determine the guidelines and what's included for clients here. For example, you can create a one-time service offering that gives clients access to you for one, 2-hour meeting, a written set of recommendations following the meeting, and email support for 7 days after the meeting to add clarity as necessary — and charge a one time fee of $500 (or $1,000, or $1,500, whatever the package demands).

Some financial advisors running practices under the monthly retainer model offer "add-on" services — like student loan analysis, or a separate accountability program — for additional flat fees. Generally speaking, any hourly fee or one-time project cost should work out to be higher per hour than your ongoing monthly retainer fee to discourage people from choosing everything a la carte, one engagement at a time.

Your goal in a monthly retainer model is to get clients into ongoing relationships, not just asking for your time with an hour here, an hour there. The difference is why ultimately the monthly retainer model is such a powerful one: monthly retainers are what's called a default-in model. Once your client becomes your client, they stay your client until they go out of their way to fire you (which, fortunately, most clients are loathe to do).

SHOULD YOU CHARGE AUM, TOO?

We've talked a lot about why AUM doesn't work for Gen X and Gen Y, and how the monthly retainer model is a much more workable, profitable solution. But it's important to understand that this discussion is specifically about an AUM-*only* model.

AUM-only models put the focus on investment management. We're focusing on comprehensive financial planning as the primary service offering. That doesn't mean you *can't* offer investment management to clients who are ready to take that step.

There can be room for charging AUM within a monthly retainer fee structure, just as there's room to offer investment management in a practice where the primary focus is comprehensive planning.

Again, you must first recognize the types of clients you work with. Some clients that you work with simply aren't going to have assets to manage, and won't have them any time soon. It doesn't make sense to roll out an offering for them because it's not a good fit. Maybe you're working with entrepreneurs, who will plow dollars back into their next business. Maybe you're working with folks with student loans and credit card issues, and they'll spend all of their available dollars just trying to knock down that debt.

But many clients *will* present at least some asset management opportunities. Even if you're not looking to manage assets now — and therefore, aren't worried about setting up an AUM model alongside a monthly retainer model — you may find that you'll evolve into it in the future as your clients grow wealth (thanks to your excellent planning advice and service!).

Should you offer it down the road? Our general answer to this is, yes I do think it makes sense to offer AUM services or plan to layer them in.

AUM won't replace your core financial planning offering, but it can compliment other services. It's an implementation service that you provide, where you can manage the investments, oversee them, and handle them on your clients' behalf.

Because asset management is not the core of the value that you provide, you won't need to do hands-on investment management work. Most advisors don't *want* to, either. Therefore, it makes sense to look at outsourcing much of the implementation work itself. Even by doing so, you can charge less for investment management than what many other financial planning firms charge because you're already being paid separately for planning services. In a world where the classic rule of thumb is a 1% AUM fee, you could decide that you only want to charge .25 basis points, .50 basis points, or .75 basis points.

You may also decide ultimately to largely outsource much of the implementation details of the management work to third-party investment firms that provide core services for this. Even so-called robo advisor services become a sensible option to partner with. At XY Planning Network, we support a partnership with Betterment Institutional to make it easier for our advisors to engage with investment management platforms in this way.

Providing financial planning on a monthly retainer basis alongside an investment management service offering that uses an AUM model makes good sense from a business perspective. It helps to grow revenue per client over time, which helps resolve the otherwise flat-fee challenge of the paying for inflating business costs in the long run. It also makes sense when you look at your client relationships over time.

If you're working with clients and effectively helping them on a path to fiscal responsibility, they will almost certainly accumulate some level of assets in an investment portfolio at some point in the future. Whether they save in a 401(k) and roll it over to you, in IRAs or outside investment accounts, or they're self employed and need someone to oversee their SEP or individual 401(k), your financial planning clients will likely obtain assets over time.

If you offer an investment management service with an AUM model as an additional benefit, that service provides a way to generate more revenue from your clients without requiring you to raise your planning fees.

THE PROFITABILITY ARGUMENT FOR AN AUM OFFERING

Imagine you start working with clients for $150 a month. You can only work with so many clients, and for the sake of argument let's say that number is 100 clients. It's simple math to see your revenue will max out at $180,000 per year. That's not a bad number by any means, but once you get to that point your business growth becomes limited.

You can hire more planners to service more clients or you can raise your fees on clients. Raising monthly fees is challenging because no one really like to go back to all of their clients and say, "I'm going to raise your financial planning fees to $160 per month (or $170 or $200)." Inevitably, your business will lose clients that would've stayed at $150 but will walk away if they're required to pay more for the same service.

Assets under management becomes a nice way to generate more revenue per client without forcing higher fees on your clients (or dealing with hiring employees — but if you do want to make hires, AUM gives you the revenue to pay for them). Let's say you have a client who receives financial planning from you at $150 per month. You've worked with them for years and over time they've accumulated $100,000. If you have an AUM model that can support them via investment management and charge .50 basis points, you'll earn an additional $500 per year through working with them. Broken down monthly, that's about $40 per month — which means your $150 monthly fee has effectively crept up closer to $200 per month without requiring you to renegotiate retainer fees with all of your clients.

Simply put, AUM fees will supplement your monthly planning fee and will help business revenue naturally rise over time.

This isn't just beneficial for your business, either — although that's certainly a great perk for many advisors. Increasing average revenue for clients also allows financial planners to reinvest in their firms and provide clients with even more services.

When your average revenue per client increases, you can hire operations staff to give clients better service. You can hire paraplanners to go deeper into the planning process with the client. Increasing average revenue per client is critical if you want to expand the depth of the services offered by your business, beyond what you can personally provide clients before you run out of bandwidth. The AUM model, working alongside a monthly retainer, is a particularly effective way to accomplish the goal of increased revenue.

DETERMINING THE EXACT

PRICE AND MONTHLY FEE

Historically, most advisors never had to formally structure pricing. Commission schedules were set and not determined by individual advisors. And the homogeneity of the AUM model and serving offering meant, at the most complex, advisors needed to determine the right minimum asset levels and percent to charge on those assets.

The rise of the monthly retainer model demands that advisors develop their own pricing mechanisms. That doesn't mean "pick a number out of the air" and determine a price for your services based on perceived value. So what should you do instead?

While we've discussed how you can charge, we haven't explained how to calculate the exact price you can charge for the services you provide. If you're unsure where to set your prices, there are a few methods you can use to calculate the answer.

Start with the Value of Your Time

The primary constraint in an advice service model is time. Your cost is the value of your time, so what is your time worth to you? Consider setting your pricing accordingly. For example, let's say that your average client will cost you 12 hours of your time per year and you want to make $150 as a professional providing service. You may want to charge $1,800 per year for the services you provide.

Here's where the monthly retainer model comes in. You can break down that large fee for your client and charge them $150 per month to work with you. This allows you to get paid what you're worth for your time and keeps professional financial services accessible to your client.

The most straightforward way to determine an exact price for your services as a professional is to estimate your time to deliver services to clients and multiple the price of your time by the number of hours you'll work. Once you determine that, your only task is to decide if you're going to bill that annually, monthly, or hourly.

And no: this is not a linear progression. Expect to go through several iterations of this process, as you grow and change and the services you provide evolve as well.

Calculate the Value of Being an Expert

It's challenging to get compensated for being an expert. You spend hundreds and thousands of hours in classrooms and conferences just to stay current with changes in the industry and that time is not looped into these fee calculations. We tend to think only about the hours that we're working for the client and not the 10,000 hours that it takes to become a master of a trade.

The problem is, the better you become, the more you undermine the hourly pricing model. For instance, the person that is a Social Security expert and can answer any

Social Security question off the top of their head within minutes is theoretically paid less than the less-knowledgeable person who needed 2 hours of thinking, research, and fact-checking to answer the same question.

You need to know the value of our own time based on the value that you can create for your client. If you save a client an hour of time and that client values an hour of *their own* time at $1,000, then the value of the service you provide to that particular client is $1,000. It's not the fact that it costs you $150 to bring it to them, it's that the time is valued by the client at $1,000.

The best way to utilize value-based pricing is to work with people who value their time at a higher level than you value yours. If you value your time at $150 per hour but you work with a client that values theirs at $500 per hour, they would gladly pay you to save them that time.

The Affordability-Based Approach

If you want to run an RIA that serves Gen X and Gen Y clients using the monthly retainer model, you likely want to provide financial planning in a way that's accessible to those clients. In that case, it always makes sense to consider the question: what can your clients *afford* to pay?

This is why the AUM model was so effective for clients who came to an advisor with existing investable assets. It served as a natural affordability model and fees were paid out of assets in an investment account. But fees in the retainer model are paid out of cash flow, which means you need to consider the incomes of the people you work with.

A business that charges firefighters and other public service workers $200 per month is doomed to fail, because these particular clients simply don't have the monthly cash flow to afford the service. That doesn't mean you can't work with these clients -- but you need to consider that what they can afford may be $100 or less per month. If, as the advisor, your want to generate a higher income for yourself, you will be required to work with clients with higher incomes. Start with what's affordable to the client and then work backwards to create a service model that still justifies your time but fits what your client can realistically afford.

Draw a Line in the Sand by Setting a Revenue Goal

Many financial advisors never sit down and determine how much they want to earn. More is not always better, either. As an entrepreneur, your earning potential is theoretically unlimited. The more you work and the better you make your business, the more you can potentially earn. You can always go from working 40 hours in a week to 60 or 80 hours and make more money.

But why? To what end? At what point will you step back and say, "Okay, I'm done, I earn enough now"? The fact that you can work more to earn more can quickly get out of hand and have you striving to reach a moving goalpost. Every time you hit the next level of income, it quickly becomes "not enough," since you can always work more and make more money.

Draw a line in the sand and set a hard revenue goal. Consider what you need and what will make you happy. You could say, "I want to make $120,000 a year. That's $10,000 per month. I have 160 hours in a month, so therefore I need to charge enough to make $63 for every hour I work."

You have to figure out how you value your time, not necessarily just what your time is worth doing something else. A lot of advisors lock in clients and fee structures that worked when you valued your time at $25 per hour, but the system falls apart when you decide your value is $250 per hour. Remember to consider that your value will likely go up over time, and plan for it.

CHAPTER 4:
IMPLEMENTING A MONTHLY RETAINER MODEL IN YOUR PRACTICE

Today, an overwhelming majority of advisors work on an AUM fee basis with a focus on investment management and financial planning thrown in as a "free" bonus for clients with assets. This inherently limits their ability to work with younger clients that don't necessarily have significant assets to manage.

The monthly retainer or subscription fee model for clients is a very different, unique business model in and of itself. Being able to go to clients and say,

"Wouldn't it be nice if you could work with a financial planner in the same way that you would any other coach or trainer, where they simply charge you an on-going fee from your credit card or bank account — the same way you pay all of your other bills?"

"You don't have to give me assets and you don't have to buy products from me. Our focus will be on creating a comprehensive financial plan for you, and guiding you to success with specific action steps and accountability. You don't have to have investments before you receive financial advice from me."

"I'm not going to sell stuff to you, I'm simply here to provide you with financial planning advice."

If you want to tell that story — the story that puts the clients needs, without conflicts of interest, ahead of your own — you need a fee-only, financial planning focused model to go with it. Using the monthly retainer model and charging people for the actual advice you give and not requiring minimum asset levels opens up a whole world of clients to work with that the rest of the industry is not looking for.

You don't necessarily want your prime differentiator to be the fees you charge. The *way* you charge is unique and it's something that sets you apart. But what you really want to differentiate on is the value and the service you provide. Really show your prospects what you do, and get specific about how you can help people like them:

"We specialize in young attorneys like you and we know how to negotiate partnership deals. And we know how to build up the savings you need for the down payment. We even know the lenders to talk to so you can finance your buy-in. And here's how we meet with our clients and work with them on an on-going basis, using a monthly retainer model. There are no sales and no commissions — you pay for the financial advice we provide, and you don't need assets in order to receive that advice. This helps eliminate conflicts of interest, since we're not incentivized to make sales, push products, or convince you to let us manage your money."

Lead with the value you provide and why it's justified with the price that you charge, and then you can point out or highlight that the nature of how you charge is unique in and of itself.

HOW TO TRANSITION FROM AN OLD BUSINESS MODEL TO THE MONTHLY RETAINER

This information on implementing a monthly retainer is all well and good if you're starting from scratch. But existing firms face a much bigger challenge, because existing models are already in place. There's a known way of doing things, and making huge changes to your fee structure isn't exactly easy.

But it is possible, and the way to do it will depend, first and foremost, on what your old model really is. We can break this into a couple of categories: transitioning from an existing hourly model, transitioning from an ongoing AUM model, and transitioning from a commission-based model.

TRANSITIONING FROM AN HOURLY MODEL

If you're going to transition from an hourly model, you have a couple of choices about how you're going to go about this — but the best, most straightforward, simple way is to reach out to your existing hourly clients and say, "we're offering a new service that we're really excited about and here's what it entails."

Then, clearly describe what your ongoing services look like for the people you work with. Set your monthly retainer price point at a place where, if they really continue to use your services one hour or a few hours at a time, it's going to be more expensive for them. The goal is to encourage clients to transition into the more stable and recurring retainer model to better serve them.

You want to make the ongoing monthly retainer option a little bit of a deal for them. Not a *huge* deal, as you don't want to take a huge cut in revenue. But remember some basics in the psychology of consumer behavior. You want people to be in an ongoing monthly retainer relationship with you. Your clients are much more likely to continue to pay you, and continue to engage your services, than when you charge them hourly and each time they must decide if their problem is worth paying for.

Any financial planner who has offered hourly services knows how difficult this is. People wait until their problems are really serious, and only then do they come in for advice because that's the point when they believe it's worth paying the hourly fee.

Additionally, the more your clients work with you, the happier they'll be with your services and the solutions you provide them. Those results make your clients even more likely to retain your services and continue working with you on an ongoing basis.

TRANSITIONING FROM AN AUM MODEL

If you're coming from an AUM model, the transition looks a little bit different. You can start with clients who are at the slightly lower end of the AUM scale for you (who were probably the least profitable for you in the first place). Your goal is to set a minimum fee per client to make sure that you're making a certain amount of revenue per client to justify financial planning services for them.

To communicate this to these clients, you don't want to just say, "we're raising our fees," or, "we're raising your minimum fee." Instead, emphasize the value of the service they'll get (because you can willingly give them the value) once you're charging them an appropriate monthly retainer fee. You might call them and say their AUM fees will shift and will include a monthly subscription fee of $100 per month — and here's all the added value and service they'll receive with that change.

That "added value and service" is all the financial planning that you likely *weren't* doing (or weren't doing consistently) because it was difficult to do with just AUM fees.

That being said, you can also position this transition as a complimentary offer. Keep your current AUM structure as is, and then go to your clients to offer financial planning in addition to investment management. Explain that it's a separate charge, but share what the service looks like and the additional value the client receives, above and beyond what they currently get from your firm.

TRANSITIONING FROM A COMMISSION MODEL

If you've been operating on a commission model, you likely have a high volume of clients and different relationships with each. Some folks you may have seen just once; you did a particular transaction with them and that was that. Others you may do business with regularly — or you may do a lot of business with, or you might just have a better personal relationship and generate referrals from them.

When you're transitioning from a commission model, you're going to have the choice and luxury of selecting the clients you want to roll this out to first. Realize that not all of your commission clients will make the switch with you just because you did business with them once with a particular product. That transaction does not mean they want comprehensive financial planning from you. So begin by making a targeted list.

Who in your client base have you done business with in the past, that you would like to have in your ongoing financial planning model? Maybe it's a collection of clients that fit your target niche. Perhaps it's clientele or people that are centers of influence or who could be good referral sources. Maybe it's just people that you enjoy working with the most and they have the financial wherewithal to pay your ongoing monthly retainer fee for the services you want to roll out.

You're going to target particular clients and go there first. Recognize that you're not going to get all of them, nor should you even try (although you can certainly communicate your offering to everyone when you roll it out). But pick the people you want to target first and reach out to them individually. Hold one-to-one meetings to let them know about the transition, what's in it for them and the value you provide, and how this change is good news, exciting. Explain the services, costs, and why it would be a good fit for them.

COMPLIANCE CONCERNS
FOR SOLO RIA OWNERS

Some of the uncertainty or pushback around using the monthly retainer model is due to compliance concerns. This is a new fee structure and regulation in the industry doesn't always keep up with growth and change. But we have hundreds of advisors in the Network who offer the monthly retainer model for their clients in state-registered, compliant RIAs.

We asked XY Planning Network's Director of Keeping Us Compliant, Scott Gill, to shed light on a few issues around the monthly retainer from a compliance standpoint.

Here's what Scott shares with us about compliance as it relates to this new business model that does an excellent job of serving Gen X and Gen Y clients:

Some states will present additional compliance burdens for firms that execute financial planning services on a "retainer." The intent is to assure fairness and transparency of client advisory fees. Regulators want to make sure that the advisor is held accountable for the work that he or she is doing, and the work must be in connection with what regulators deem to be a reasonable fee.

Retainers for professional services can include circumstances in which professionals are paid despite the fact that their services are not utilized. For example, an attorney may be paid on retainer for their availability, but if no legal matters arise for the client, then the attorney may never actually work for the fee. This is obviously impermissible for financial planning and investment management services in the view of most state regulators.

The burden of proof is on the advisor to prove that they completed the work to merit the fee. With the more traditional AUM model of financial planning business, regulators have a firm method by which they can test that clients' needs are being met and annual advisory account reviews are being completed. Regulators have been a little sluggish to keep up with updates in the industry in regards to newer and changing business models (including the monthly retainer).

Some states require you to make arrangements for fee payments to be held in escrow and have an independent third-party to make disbursements from the escrow account if you use language like "retainer" in your ADV. Clearly, this is an additional compliance burden that most firms would rather avoid. In states that hold this preference, it's usually sufficient to utilize the term "fixed fee" in place of the word "retainer" to avoid any additional regulatory scrutiny.

This option involves disclosing fees as a fixed fee, paid monthly or quarterly, with a 12 month commitment. This payment option mirrors the retainer model without the language that may create regulatory red flags.

In communicating with various state regulators, we found that a majority of states allow the use of the monthly retainer model. But the area that generates the most regulatory interest around this specific fee structure is custody.

To give you an example, one state declares that if a firm will be accepting prepayment of advisory fees more than 6 months in advance and for more than $1,200 per client, the firm must maintain at all times a positive net worth and must show this through its financials. While the majority of states forego escrow requirements, many do impose additional compliance regulations if the RIA collects fees in excess of $500 more than 6 months in advance.

Full custody is triggered when a firm requires or solicits prepayment of more than $500 in fees per client 6 months in advance — and that adds more and extremely costly compliance responsibilities. Firms with custody often must undergo custody audits that require firm owners to hire independent accountants to conduct an annual audit of their firm.

This is where the monthly retainer can benefit you from a compliance standpoint. By charging monthly, financial planners can stretch out the payments over the course of the year, avoiding the need to solicit prepayment of more than $500 in fees six months in advance.

When it comes to any issues or questions surrounding compliance, the best practice is to always document, document, document. Each time you contact a client or complete work on a client's financial profile, document it in some fashion. An effective CRM that captures the date, time, and notes from each client interaction can be critical towards maintaining evidence of regulator work executed on a client's financial plan.

Scott is a licensed Securities Principal with experience in both RIA and broker-dealer compliance. He began his financial services career in 2006 as a Registered Representative with E*Trade Financial in Alpharetta, Georgia. He has also worked with J.P. Morgan Private Banking in Chicago, Illinois and with Wells Fargo Advisors in Chapel Hill, North Carolina.

Scott is a graduate of The University of North Carolina at Chapel Hill and holds FINRA Series 7, 63, 65, 24, 4 and 53 Licenses. He currently lives in Charlotte with his wife, Meredith, and their two sons, Tyson and Jackson.

CHAPTER 5:
DEALING
WITH A MORE
DIFFICULT SALE

Even when you can see the benefits of the monthly retainer model, there's still a big hangup that many financial advisors have: selling this method of charging for financial planning advice feels more difficult than other fee structures. And this makes sense when you consider that advisors have historically sold investment management or other insurance or investment products. It feels simple to sit down in a prospect meeting and explain that as the advisor, you'll manage clients' investments with a fancy investment strategy that will "get the upside and manage the downside risk."

It's easy to justify AUM fees for million-dollar clients. Who wouldn't pay 1% to a professional who promises to protect the other 99% of the clients' wealth? As an industry, we feel more comfortable selling other fee models because it feels as if they justify themselves. There's a tangible value if you manage assets and those assets provide the client with a return over time.

Financial planning as a standalone service *is* a lot harder to sell. We're talking about intangible value. The real value in financial planning is peace of mind, accountability, and professional guidance. It's standing between your client and a big mistake, as Carl Richards puts it. (Another way Carl phrases it: financial planning is about managing behavior, not necessarily managing money.)

For us as advisors and educated professionals, it's obvious that our role provides immense value for the client who might not otherwise save, invest, stay on track, or avoid pitfalls of the market. But the challenge is *showing* prospects and clients that value.

And because financial planning in general has always presented a challenge in terms of selling, we've traditionally thrown in that service with investment management as a freebie. The industry has thrived on selling complexity via investments and insurance — and including financial planning like it's a bonus for the client.

Working on a monthly retainer model to provide comprehensive financial planning as a core service offering means separating these two elements of our work. We can offer financial planning *and* investment management as two separate services. As such, they come with .two separate fees. What's important to realize is that it's not the monthly retainer that is difficult to sell. For most advisors, it's selling the value of financial planning as that stand-alone service.

HOW DO YOU SELL FINANCIAL PLANNING AS A STANDALONE SERVICE?

How do you convince clients of your value when your pricing is transparent? The short answer: make your value transparent as well. In practice, that means you must paint a picture for clients (or prospective clients) of what you'll do for them. Your explanation of your value needs to be incredibly tangible and concrete for anyone coming in the door. What are the benefits of working with you? What outcomes can you provide? What are you actually going to *do*, and what actions will you take together?

Answering these questions requires that *you* understand the value of financial planning. Advisors must absolutely believe that the value of the financial planning they provide is worth what that client is going to pay for it. Here's the good news: financial advisors who provide comprehensive financial planning services for $100 to $200 per month give clients *thousands* of dollars of value in exchange.

And the more focused your niche that you serve, the easier it is to answer these questions. You can answer in terms specific and relevant to your niche. It's easier to sell specific planning services to specific people than differentiating generalist planning services to a generalized breadth of prospects.

Say you have a client who works as an anesthesiologist with a rising premium disability policy. As part of the planning you provide, you research their benefits and help them make a switch to a level premium or a fixed premium disability policy. That change saves the client $160,000 over the next 30 years of his career. That one simple switch pays for the rest of your relationship over the same amount of time!

If you start outlining all the ways you help clients and save them money — and help them live better lives and reach the goals that are most important to them — you can sell your financial planning services better.

CONSIDER THE CONSUMER PERSPECTIVE

If you're worried about selling the idea of financial planning services billed as a monthly fee, take a step back. Consider that, while this way of structuring your fees feels brand-new and maybe even a little bizarre to you, consumers don't have the same context for analyzing this method of charging for advice.

You may be the first advisor a next generation client has ever worked with, so they don't know any different than the fee structure you present. They don't know the history of financial planning fee models and probably don't even know what "AUM" means. This isn't meant to discount the intelligence of Gen X and Gen Y clients, but simply to point out that they don't live in this industry. This is not knowledge they deeply understand because they don't work in this space. You do, and your perspective on industry history, issues, and changes is radically different. So when you tell a client that they'll pay you the same way they pay every other bill that they ever pay, they say, "okay." You offer a monthly subscription just like most other services they want and pay.

All this being said, there are also specific strategies you can implement to help you communicate value to clients. These will help you take a service that can offer intangible, hard-to-explain value and frame what you do in more concrete terms so prospects can quickly grasp exactly why they need to work with you — and why your monthly fee makes your skill and expertise affordable and accessible, so hiring you becomes a no-brainer.

USE A CLIENT SERVICE CALENDAR

If you're going to work with clients on a monthly basis throughout the year, show them what you're likely to do for them throughout that entire year. A client service calendar is a great way to illustrate those benefits, outcomes, and actions you need to communicate.[5] This gives you a simple way to show what your clients can expect on a month-to-month basis.

Remember that when financial advisors say things like, "I'm going to provide financial planning services for you," consumers don't understand what that means — or what it actually looks like, in real life, in practice. Younger consumers may be especially in the dark about what "financial planning services" entail.

It's not always easy, but put yourself in the shoes of where your clients are. These may be clients who have never engaged with an advisor and aren't familiar with the financial services industry. These are people who simply don't know what financial planning is all about. They're a clean slate and you have to explain to them what it is you do and how you provide value that is congruent with the fee you charge.

ENGAGE IN PERSUASIVE CONVERSATION BY TELLING STORIES

Another way you can vividly illustrate and explain your value when you use the monthly retainer model is by telling stories. And no, that's not a cute way of saying lie or stretch the truth. Storytelling is a very powerful way to explain and illustrate your values. You might explain a specific course

---

[5] https://www.kitces.com/blog/crafting-an-annual-client-service-calendar-to-illustrate-a-financial-planners-value-to-prospective-clients/

of action by describing another client in a similar situation. Here's an example of a story that helps your prospect or client get present to the value of your services:

> "We have another client that's in a similar situation to where you are right now, and we've been working with them over the past year to help them reach their goals. Here's what we've been doing together. When they had the opportunity to change jobs, we sat down and helped them evaluate the job offer. We talked through how they could go back and make a counter offer for a better deal that would put them further ahead financially. We helped them go through all of the employee benefits enrollments and paperwork in the new job. We reviewed their tax returns for tax planning opportunities at the end of the year. We helped them roll over an old 401k when they left their old job and helped them get set up with the options in their new 401k."

Storytelling allows you to paint a clear picture of the actions you can take. It's difficult to say exactly what you'll do for prospects walking in the door, because you don't know what their specific situation is. But you still need to lay out the value you provide and how that lines up with your fee structure. It's much easier to explain what you've done for other clients who share similarities with the prospect.

This is yet another why it is so important to have a niche, too. The more clearly defined your niche is — the more common the problems are of your clients — the easier it is to tell these stories and have a very detailed and focused client service calendar.[6] It makes it easier to know exactly what a prospect needs before they give you their entire history and all the details of where they are, where they want to go, and what they need help with along the way. You can tell that story. You can make marketing materials to explain it further. You can show your target audience what it is that they can get from you to justify your value.

PULL ANALOGIES FROM OTHER INDUSTRIES

Most consumers deal with some degree of confusion when thinking about the financial services industry. There's no regulation around the terms "financial advisor" or "financial planner," and the average person isn't likely to inherently understand the differences between distinctions like fee-only and fee-based. That confusion, or lack of understanding, makes it challenging to explain your value using terms that we as advisors feel comfortable and familiar with. What's obvious to you about the industry as someone who is in it is *not* so clear for others who don't understand all the ins and outs.

Instead of trying to use terminology and jargon from our profession, explain your value to prospects by using language they *do* understand. Pull analogies from other industries. One that tends to work well is to talk about your value in the context of medicine and doctors.

---

[6] https://www.kitces.com/sample-annual-client-service-calendar-gen-x-gen-y-monthly-retainer-clientele/

We pay for our health insurance on a monthly basis so that our doctors visits are covered. We're essentially pre-paying our doctors visits in the form of a monthly fee for our insurance. We don't see the doctor every month and we don't expect to. In fact, we might only see the doctor once a year.

But part of the reason we pay for health insurance is so that if we need the doctor, it's covered as a part of the ongoing monthly fee paid indirectly through health insurance. That fee remains flat and predictable no matter what we need medical attention for: from little things like calling to ask questions about a minor issue all the way to extreme situations when we need the doctor for a serious problem that's time-consuming and would otherwise be very expensive for us.

You can have a static, set list of services that are always provided and will hopefully provide value. But in many cases, the biggest value comes from the fact that your clients have a relationship with a professional who will take care of their financial needs in the same way a doctor takes care of medical needs. It's all access to subscription-based programs that give clients access to professionals when they need it.

While you should have a very good idea of the list of financial planning problems and questions your clients will walk in the door with, you don't necessarily need to know exactly *which* problems and questions from that list they'll likely need help with to explain your value. Doctors don't know what their patients will come in needing care for. But you can list whatever problems are common within your niche of clients, explain that these are the issues that come up often and you as the professional are prepared to deal with any and all of them.

A monthly fee allows your clients access no matter what problems arise, whether they're more complex or unique to their specific situation. You are available for them as their lives ebb and flow, as they experience ups and downs. You won't charge more because a problem occurred or something unexpected came up or a more challenging issue arose.

Explaining your value in terms of service models that clients are already familiar with and already accept will help close the gap and help them understand. It's not always easy to close the sale when you're so transparent with your pricing, but it's possible when you can speak in the clients' language to clearly lay out the support, guidance, and care you provide.

CHAPTER 6:
CASE STUDIES

*HOW THE MONTHLY RETAINER
MODEL WORKS IN PRACTICE*

ANJALI JARIWALA OF
FIT ADVISORS

Founder of: FIT Advisors

Website: fitadvisors.com

LinkedIn: linkedin.com/
in/anjalijayakumar

Twitter: twitter.com/AnjaliFIT

Anjali Jariwala started her career in tax at PwC as a CPA. She worked with the company for a little over 6 years before realizing she was ready for a change — but wasn't sure what to do next. Around the same time, she says, her husband was in the process of earning his MBA and took a financial planning class taught by a local fee only advisor. Her husband suggest Jariwala look into financial planning, and she talked with the same advisor who taught the class.

"It seemed like a good fit and I took the plunge," says Jariwala. "I quit my job and started interning with a firm while studying for the CFP®. After passing the exam, I took a job with a very large RIA in Chicago that targeted ultra high net worth baby boomers." She says that was a great learning experience, but not the niche she wanted to serve long-term. "I started researching and interviewing with local fee-only firms, but could not find one that did not impose a minimum AUM or would allow me to serve a younger population," she explains. "I came across XYPN and after encouragement from co-founder Alan Moore and founding member Sophia Bera of Gen Y Planning, I decided to launch my own firm."

We talked more with Jariwala about her experience in starting her own firm, running a monthly retainer model, and her advice for other financial advisors looking for ways to profitably serve Gen X and Gen Y in fee-only financial planning.

XYPN: What were your early experiences like in starting your firm? How did you find and develop a niche?

Anjali Jariwala: I launched my firm in June 2015. There are struggles with all stages of the process. In the beginning, it was the pressure of bringing on clients and getting to cash flow neutral. Then the struggles shifted to running a business, putting processes in place, and everything else that goes with being an entrepreneur.

I have to say, the process does not necessarily get easier just the responsibilities change. When going through the compliance and getting things up and running, I initially wanted to focus on physicians since my husband is one and I have experience on their specific needs. But when I launched I was eager to just bring in revenue, so I marketed myself as an advisor serving the needs of "Gen X professionals" as to not exclude anyone who may be interested.

Since this was so broad, I was getting prospects across the spectrum and realized it would be difficult to scale my business long term and develop the necessary expertise if I continued to serve such a broad niche. In October 2015, I rebranded my firm and myself to focus solely on physicians and business owners. That made a huge difference in my practice.

The quality of my prospects improved significantly in that those who signed up for a consultation were already within my niche so our conversation was focused on their needs and it was easier to convert prospects to clients.

XYPN: Did you start your firm with the monthly retainer model as your fee structure?

AJ: I started with this model, but I did change the language in conversations I was having with clients. Initially,

I explained the fee structure as a monthly retainer. Now, I talk about it in terms of an annual retainer that I bill either monthly or quarterly based on the client's preference.

Many of the Gen X prospects I spoke with did not understand the monthly retainer model. They assumed paying monthly meant receiving services on a monthly basis, which is not necessarily the case. When I changed the description to an annual retainer that I bill monthly, that seemed to resonate much better.

XYPN: Do you use another fee model in addition to the monthly retainer?

AJ: I charge an annual retainer for financial planning and an AUM fee for investment management so I am able to serve clients who may not have that much in assets yet. I did have a start-up offering when I first launched that I charged a flat fee for. As I've gotten busier, I've phased out that service.

XYPN: What do you currently charge for your services?

AJ: I charge a one-time onboarding fee of $1,500 which covers the first 2 months of service. I then charge an annual retainer (billed monthly or quarterly). The annual retainer is $2,400 for a single person and $3,600 for a married couple. My fees for investment management are 0.75% on the first $1M and 0.5% afterward.

XYPN: Why is a monthly retainer so powerful for profitably serving Gen X and Gen Y clients?

AJ: It allows individuals who do not have certain minimum level of assets to hire a fee-only advisor. It's unfortunate that many fee only advisors require a certain minimum like $250,000. By the time someone acquires that, they may be much older. I honestly believe the earlier you can get someone in place to help, the better off you will be over the long run — so younger clients need a financial advisor now, not when they're 50 or 60 years old.

I also find that Gen X and Gen Y clients are eager to find someone to help them and many of the service models out there consist of people who sell them commissioned products or funds with high expense ratios.

XYPN: How do you position your value as an advisor to your clients and prospects?

AJ: I emphasize that I am both a CPA and CFP® so I bring heavy tax planning to the process. I stress the importance of working as a fee-only advisor and being a fiduciary. But at the end of the day, I never pressure anyone to use me.

I tell all prospects that the decision is very personal, and that they should pick someone that not only can serve their needs from a technical perspective but also who they feel comfortable with. If that person is me, great! If not, I completely understand. I try to be as honest and open with prospects.

There is a huge advantage in being different in this industry. Unfortunately, there's not much diversity in the current market of fee-only advisors — which is misaligned with the diverse pool of people who are seeking an advisor. Many times the decision will come down to who the prospect felt like they had a connection with. If you are able to relate to them personally, that provides instant trust. If you are different from the crowd, emphasize that because you will draw in prospects that way.

XYPN: Do you have any advice for other financial advisors considering starting their own businesses?

AJ: I recommend having enough in savings to last for at least 1 year if not more. The business will take longer than you expect to be profitable and you do not want money to be the main driving factor of your business decisions. Don't feel like you have to get 100% of your processes in place, either. Try to get the main things up and running, launch and learn as you go.

I also recommend figuring out a niche as early in your process as you can and try very hard to stick to it, even if that means your growth is a bit slower in the beginning. In order to help from a cash flow perspective, offer some sort of quick start program but reserve your monthly retainer clients for your niche.

XYPN: Any tips on setting monthly retainer fees?

AJ: I encourage people to be thoughtful about the fees they set and try not to underprice the value you will provide. It's very difficult to increase fees so you want to set them at a level that you feel compensates you for your time.

ERIC ROBERGE OF BEYOND YOUR HAMMOCK

Founder of:
Beyond Your Hammock

Website:
beyondyourhammock.com

LinkedIn:
linkedin.com/in/ericroberge

Twitter:
twitter.com/beyondfinances

Eric Roberge graduated from Babson College, a business school known for its focus on entrepreneurship. He majored in finance and started the early part of his career working for several large investment institutions in the mutual fund arena.

After 6 years, Roberge realized the corporate world wasn't for him. He sought to connect with a career that better aligned with the life he wanted to live, which lead to working as an independent financial advisor under several different broker dealers.

Although he gained valuable experience taking this path, Roberge eventually decided to create his own financial planning firm to truly achieve his goal. He founded Beyond Your Hammock, an RIA that focuses on serving professionals and entrepreneurs in their 30s.

Roberge is one of Investment News' 40 Under 40 for 2016, and he was named one of the top 10 CFPs under 36 by Wealth Management Magazine. He's also been named to Financial Advisor Magazine's list of Top 10 Young Advisors to Watch. He frequently speaks to professional financial associations and groups, including the FPA, NAPFA, and fi360 about how financial advisors can work with next generation clients.

We chatted with Roberge to better understand his business and how he helps clients simplify the complex world of personal finance to see things from a new perspective

XYPN: Tell us more about your firm. How did you start, and how has your business changed over time?

Eric Roberge: I launched BYH in the summer of 2013, fresh off my first FPA NexGen Gathering where I connected with others also starting their own fee-only RIAs. I had been thinking about implementing a monthly retainer model for a long time to serve young professionals, and this was my opportunity to make that a reality.

The early months as a business owner were very difficult as I made little to no money. The good thing about the monthly retainer model is that it allows young people to work with a financial advisor, *and* also allows the advisor to build their own much needed recurring income stream.

I didn't bring on my first client until 4 months after I launched, but then experienced a great amount of growth in the following year. It was exciting and also challenging because I was able to choose the people that I wanted to work with, but also had to create a new process for this type of business model and type of client, on the fly.

Looking back I've come a long way. In almost 3 years, my firm looks vastly different than it did when I began. I have a framework, a process, and a lot of great clients that I love working with. I'm also beginning to look for someone to hire to support further business growth.

XYPN: What encouraged you to try the monthly retainer model as your fee structure?

ER: The revenue models that were built to support older, wealthy clients created a problem in this industry for those of us wanting to serve next generation clients. Since my focus is young professionals and entrepreneurs, I needed to design a revenue model that allowed me to provide comprehensive support in a way that didn't tie my business earnings to client assets.

Just before I launched my firm, I was experimenting with one-time planning fees and I quickly realized that model wasn't viable for the long term. The monthly retainer model seemed to solve both of these problems — I didn't have to charge clients AUM, and it allowed me to generate sustainable business revenue.

XYPN: Do you also use another fee model in your practice?

ER: Yes. My focus is providing comprehensive financial planning for my clients. For that, I charge with the monthly retainer model. However, I also have clients with investable assets. I charge a separate, AUM-based fee to manage money for those clients.

As I continue to work with my clients, they will grow their wealth and therefore have additional money to manage. At some point, they'll have enough assets to allow me to convert them from a monthly retainer to a strictly AUM-based model.

The greatest thing about the monthly retainer model is that it allows me to help the upwardly mobile professionals achieve wealth faster. It really fills a gap and makes planning accessible for people who aren't wealthy — yet.

XYPN: Why is a monthly retainer so powerful for profitably serving Gen X and Gen Y clients?

ER: For one thing, it allows this age group to access comprehensive financial planning, which they typically can't find at their asset level. It also allows business owners to build recurring revenue streams without limiting who they can work with.

XYPN: Are there drawbacks that other advisors should be aware of before they implement this kind of fee structure in their RIAs?

ER: The downside to the monthly retainer model is that it can't serve *everybody*. The challenge is to be able to provide value for an appropriate fee and still achieve a profit in your business.

Because of this, clients need to have a certain level of income to make it all worthwhile for both parties. The client needs to be able to afford the service, and the advisor needs to get paid for the value they add.

XYPN: How do you communicate your value to prospects and clients?

ER: I tell my clients that I'm a personal trainer for their finances. Just like an effective physical training regimen, I provide my clients with a framework within which we create an action plan geared toward their goals. Along with organizing their finances and clearly defining those goals, I also hold them accountable to taking the actions necessary to get there.

This type of relationship allows clients to make intelligent decisions and avoid costly mistakes which will help them grow their wealth over time.

XYPN: What would you tell another advisor who's considering trying the monthly retainer model?

ER: Although this model is viable inside of an existing firm, you really do have to go all in to make it effective.

Whether it's you or one of your employees, someone must focus on implementing the process and making adjustments to fit your firm's values and overall vision.

For advisors who are starting from scratch, it's extremely important to research and implement outside income streams while you grow the business.

Without a separate source of income — from a side gig or savings account — you will not be able to provide effective service. That's because a lack of income shifts your focus onto your own well being instead of that of your clients. It takes your attention away from their needs and the needs of your business.

XYPN: Is there any advice you'd give to other advisors running their own RIA in general?

ER: It's important to develop a clear vision and think outside the box about how to create a business that works for both you and your clients. Anything is possible in this industry.

It's up to us to improve the public's view of how financial advisors help others. To do that, we need to provide effective service and transparency. Overall, we need to do what is in the best interest of our clients. Ultimately, any revenue model is secondary to doing what is right.

DANIEL WRENNE OF WRENNE FINANCIAL PLANNING

Founder of:
Wrenne Financial Planning

Website:
wrennefinancial.com

LinkedIn:
linkedin.com/company/
wrenne-financial-planning-llc

Twitter:
twitter.com/wrennefinancial

Daniel Wrenne entered the financial planning profession through a big insurance company, and worked there for almost 9 years. He focused mostly on young physicians and sold life and disability insurance and investments.

When he eventually left, it was to start his own financial planning firm. His RIA, Wrenne Financial Planning, launched in October, 2014. Wrenne brought his experience in serving doctors to his new business, but left the sales behind. He now provides fee-only financial planning services to young physicians.

He uses the monthly retainer in his firm because he feels it's the most conflict-free way to serve the clients who rely on him for comprehensive advice. We talked with Wrenne to get more details on his business and how he profitably serves a niche within the next generation demographic.

XYPN: What were your early experiences like when you launched your firm — and how does your business look today?

DW: We opened the firm November, 2014 — and the first 6 months were pure chaos. I brought over 50 or so clients from my old firm. Getting them all up to speed while also managing a flow of new clients was crazy.

Fortunately, I have a rockstar employee in my assistant, Jen. She helps with administrative work in the firm, and does a lot of paraplanning work. She's studying for her CFP now and acing all the pre-tests!

XYPN: What does your client base look like?

DW: We have around 70 monthly retainer clients, 10 investment management only clients, and around 10 hourly clients. 75% are young medical professionals.

We offer a baseline financial planning service that consists of delivering annual financial plans and on-call service throughout the year. And we have several add-on services that clients can use. These might include student loan planning, cash flow management, investment management, and help shopping for and managing insurance.

XYPN: What do you currently charge for your services?

DW: The basic financial planning service for most clients is $750 upfront and $150 per month ongoing. Add-on services range in price, depending on the service and client.

The student loan service, for example, is an additional $30 to $50 per month. If it's standalone, we add an upfront fee starting at $399.

For AUM, we charge 1% at most (and that declines with assets). We also offer a full service option for $750 up front and $400 per month ongoing. This gives clients the basic planning with all the add-on services. Our average household pays $2,900 for financial planning services per year.

XYPN: Why is a monthly retainer so powerful for profitably serving Gen X and Gen Y clients?

DW: The monthly retainer model is extremely transparent and predictable. It cuts out most the conflict. It allows us to stay extremely informed about their circumstances and positions us to easily answer one-off questions throughout the year that would typically be difficult without good info.

Plus, young people are used to monthly payments. It spreads the bigger fees out.

XYPN: Are there any downsides to the monthly retainer model?

DW: It doesn't work well for people that want everything done for them at a low price. It also doesn't work well for people that don't want an ongoing advisor. And the fact that it *is* so transparent can scare people off.

XYPN: How do you position your value as an advisor to your clients and prospects?

DW: I am their objective source for money advice. I also happen to fully understand their financial situation and am unemotional about it. I save them time, provide expert advice, and behavior coaching. Not to mention, this process initiates long-range planning that is so important yet often overlooked — so that's something I explain to illustrate value, too.

XYPN: Do you have any advice for other financial advisors considering implementing a monthly retainer model in their practice?

DW: Do it now. It's the future of financial planning. Eventually you will be forced to implement it into your practice to stay competitive.

PAMELA J. HORACK OF PATHFINDER PLANNING AND YOUR FINANCIAL MOM

Founder of:
Pathfinder Planning

Website:
pathfinderplanningllc.com

LinkedIn:
linkedin.com/in/pamhorack

Twitter:
twitter.com/urfinancialmom

Pam Horack is a a fee-only financial planner who founded Pathfinder Planning and counts herself as the "financial mom" of her clients. She's there for the people she serves by supporting their dreams. Horack provides guidance, takes away the stress of making financial decisions alone, and ensures her advice is in the best interest of her clients.

Horack says her pre-mom life always involved money in some fashion: she held many jobs in financial services, and all her roles saw her training and managing teams. All the while, people around her always had financial questions that they sought her help on — and she tried her best to guide them to sound answers.

Horack spent time away from work after having her two children, but eventually returned to financial services — this time, by getting into financial planning and opening her own firm. A founding member of XY Planning Network, she shared her experiences in running a fee-only financial planning firm that offers a monthly retainer model.

XYPN: Tell us more about your firm. When did you start, and how has your fee structure evolved over time?

Pam Horack: I started in 2010, before the retainer model was really in play. I began by charging an hourly fee, but quickly found that I was terrible at estimating. I would give a price range on my contracts and always charged the maximum, even though I put in far more hours than I had originally thought. Tracking the hours was a hassle, too.

I switched to a one-time fee for service. This worked better, but then I found I was still doing work for clients for months before the engagement was complete with no cash flow to support that time in-between their first and final payment.

After that, I changed (again!) to an up-front fee coupled with a monthly retainer. Since the bulk of the work if done in the beginning, my revenues better reflect the amount I work I actually put into a plan. Some clients still want the one-time fee for service, and that's okay. For those that want continued help, the retainer model seems to work well.

XYPN: What other fee structures do you use in addition to your monthly retainer offering?

PH: In 2015, I added asset management through Betterment Institutional to my practice. While most of my clients continue to use Vanguard and Fidelity, Betterment is a good choice for those who are novice investors who want someone to manage their money. I typically charge AUM less than 1% for these services in addition to my planning retainer.

I also provide group educational classes on occasion and charge separately for those. I'm looking into providing an online class coupled with one-hour of planning as well. I believe I can reach a larger mass of people with these services and diversify my revenue stream in the process.

XYPN: Why does a monthly retainer work so well for Gen X and Gen Y clients?

PH: I believe that this group is used to receiving service for a fee. By breaking up a large fee into monthly payments, they are better able to budget and pay for this service. Also, monthly retainers help to build a relationship that would otherwise not exist.

Consider a financial "transaction." When complete, a young person or someone with few assets often never hears from the "advisor" again to rebalance or review. They would never even know if that person is still employed as they are often shuffled from one person to another at a brokerage or wire house.

XYPN: Are there any elements to the monthly retainer model that *don't* work so well?

PH: There is always the "pain of payment" that happens with this model. Each month when the client makes their payment, they may ask: *what is the value I'm getting from this? Should I keep paying it?* You have to stay in front of them to show your value.

Another downside is collections. While they are few and far between, businesses need to create processes and guidelines for clients who are still under contract but decide not to pay anymore.

XYPN: How do you position your value as an advisor to your clients and prospects?

PH: When I told people that I was a financial planner, they would say, "Oh – so you sell insurance." I knew then I needed to be able to explain what I did for clients so they could wrap their heads around the process. So, I created my approach to planning, where I explain my Financial Planning Tower.[7]

Once I show this graphic and explain how it works, everyone gets it. Then, it's a matter of them deciding if my services are right for them. I review my contract, which answers many of their questions, and encourage them to come on board. Sometimes prospects want just a one time-plan, and that's okay. For those that need ongoing help, the payment structure really helps make planning affordable.

---

[7] http://www.pathfinderplanningllc.com/planning-packages.html

And even if a prospect doesn't sign up, I have at least educated them on the big picture of how they can get their finances in order.

XYPN: Do you have any advice for other financial advisors considering implementing this in their practice?

PH: Know yourself. Do you really want to educate, encourage, and help the average person? Offering planning and dealing with the minutiae of budgeting and some hand-holding isn't for everyone. You may be more inclined to manage assets or build and monitor portfolios. Decide which direction is best for you from a personal standpoint.

You should also plan to outsource at least some of what you're doing. If you are an existing firm looking to expand into a younger market, you may have some internal cultural hurdles to overcome. It may be to your benefit to outsource the planning or hire someone to build that type of business within your firm. A business-within-a-business, so to speak. This can help add value to your firm as you think about succession planning.

And don't forget to research. Study upcoming trends, ask tons of questions, review software and ask more questions. Contact other advisors who have already successfully implemented a monthly retainer plan. And did I say ask questions? Keep on asking until you are comfortable with the direction you want to go within your firm.

CHAPTER 7:
ADDITIONAL RESOURCES AND INFORMATION

We hope this book provided the introduction, overview, actionable advice, and useful instruction you need to fully utilize the monthly retainer model and know why it's a key piece to solving the puzzle of profitably serving the next generation.

But of course, no matter how solid of a resource it is, no one book can contain all the nuanced information or tactical how-tos we *could* talk about when helping people design firms that operate on a monthly retainer model to serve Gen X and Gen Y clients. If you're looking for additional support, we're happy to point you in the right direction to give you all the tools you need to understand, implement, and use this fee structure in a successful practice.

FURTHER READING

We suggest checking out these books and blogs to help flush out your knowledge around financial planning for the next generation and the monthly retainer model:

- Nerd's Eye View (https://www.kitces.com)

- XYPN's Advisor Blog (http://www.xy-planningnetwork.com/advisor/blog)

- Behavior Gap (http://www.behaviorgap.com)

- So You Want to Be a Financial Planner (https://www.amazon.com/So-You-Want-Financial-Planner/dp/0985259426)

ENJOY MORE ENGAGEMENT

Ready to move beyond reading? Finding communities where you can engage and interact with like-minded people working toward similar goals is a critical component to success in business. Start with these resources:

- XYPN Radio (https://itunes.apple.com/us/podcast/xypn-radio/id1031713236?mt=2)

- XYPN Radio VIP Community (http://xyplanningnetwork.com/vip)

- Events for financial advisors, including conferences, open calls, meetups, and more: http://www.xyplanningnetwork.com/advisor/events

- The Best Conferences for Financial Advisors (2016 Edition): https://www.kitces.com/blog/the-12-best-conferences-for-top-financial-advisors-to-choose-from-in-2016

- National Association of Personal Financial Advisors, or NAPFA (https://www.napfa.org)

LEARN MORE ABOUT XY PLANNING NETWORK

If you're fully committed to building out a financial planning firm for Gen X and Gen Y clients or want the education you need to incorporate next generation clients and planning into your existing practice, consider getting the full support of XY Planning Network on your side.

Membership costs only $397 per month for financial advisors and solo RIA owners. Corporate memberships are available for $797 per month for multiple advisors to access the Network and all our platforms.

Financial advisors who want to start their own firms can do so in an extremely cost-effective way and surrounded by a community of peers and professionals dedicated to their success. New firms can take advantage of an initial RIA registration package and receive compliance support, a strong community and knowledge base to answer questions and solve problems along the way, and a turnkey technology platform that provides everything needed for new firms to run and grow efficiently.

Membership includes access to the following technology stack:

- Advizr

- Arkovi

- Message Watcher

- Pay Simple

- PreciseFP

- TD Ameritrade

- Wealthbox

- Betterment

- NAPFA Membership

- Kitces Report

- Bob Veres' Insider Information

- Financial Planner's Assistance

- Markel Cambridge

Members also enjoy additional discounts with technologies like:

- 99Designs

- Balance Financial

- Blueleaf

- Guide Financial

- inStream

- Wealth Solutions

- Money Guide Pro

- Ruby Receptionist

- Best Bequest

- Blooom

- BNA Tax Prep

- ComConnect File Sync

- Jive Communication

- Kwanti

- My Plan Map

- Right Capital

- Riskalyze

- College for Financial Planning

- Financial Advisor Bean Counters

We're constantly adding new partners to our technology stack, and we're a member-driven Network. That means if there's a tech tool that you want to use as a member, let us know. We'll work on securing new integrated and discounted partnerships.

Existing firm owners can benefit from ongoing compliance support with compliance experts available to answer questions anytime. XYPN also makes it possible to run a fee-only financial planning firm with less overhead. Membership offers thousands of dollars worth of value via the turnkey technology platform detailed above, compliance support, marketing resources, and more — like one-on-one conversations from experts in the forums, group coaching, exclusive educational resources, and members-only webinars.

You also get continuing compliance support as your business grows and changes over time. Receive answers and information when you want to hire new advisors in your firm, register your RIA in new states to serve more clients, and try new service models to increase profitability. You also have an exclusive, members-only forum that you can use to bring your questions to our compliance experts.

Corporate members will enjoy tapping into the collective knowledge of a group of advisors who are successfully serving Gen X and Gen Y clients. You can engage with smaller firms to discuss and evaluate various iterations of new business models, which allows your business to learn and grow without the tedious trial and error. And you'll also receive education on how to market to and retain next generation clients. You can access a library of resources to better position your firm for Gen X and Gen Y, and to understand how to reach that demographic through content and inbound marketing.

Of course, this is just a small sampling of the full list of member benefits XYPN provides to financial advisors who join the Network. We're constantly pushing to expand what we offer and provide to members and always seeking new partnerships and discounts for those in our organization to enjoy.

If you'd like to learn more about how XY Planning Network can support you, join us for our next Intro Webinar at http://xyplanningnetwork.com/webinar.

You can also get further details at http://xyplanningnetwork.com/advisor and we invite you to connect with us on social media. Tweet us @xyplanning or follow us on Facebook at http://facebook.com/xyplanningnetwork.

We look forward to connecting with you soon!

— Michael Kitces and Alan Moore
Co-Founders, XY Planning Network